Sincerely Yours
Writing Your Own Letter

by Nancy Loewen   illustrated by Christopher Lyles

PiCTURE WiNDOW BOOKS
Minneapolis, Minnesota

Editor: Jill Kalz
Designer: Nathan Gassman
Page Production: Melissa Kes
Editorial Director: Nick Healy
The illustrations in this book were created
with mixed media on illustration board.

Picture Window Books
151 Good Counsel Drive
P.O. Box 669
Mankato, MN 56002-0669
877-845-8392
www.picturewindowbooks.com

Printed in the United States of America, North Mankato, MN.

 All books published by Picture Window Books
are manufactured with paper containing at least
10 percent post-consumer waste.

Library of Congress Cataloging-in-Publication Data
Loewen, Nancy, 1964-
Sincerely yours : writing your own letter /
by Nancy Loewen ; illustrated by Christopher Lyles.
p. cm. — (Writer's Toolbox)
Includes index.
ISBN 978-1-4048-5338-6 (library binding)
ISBN 978-1-4048-5339-3 (paperback)
1. Letter writing—Juvenile literature.
2. English language—Composition and
exercises—Juvenile literature. I. Lyles,
Christopher, 1977- II. Title.
PE1495.L64 2009
808.6—dc22   2008040589

092009-005611R

Special thanks to our adviser, Terry Flaherty, Ph.D., Professor of
English, Minnesota State University, Mankato, for his expertise.

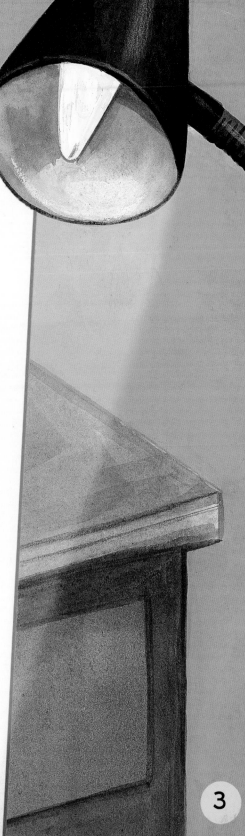

Dear Reader,

Suppose you lived 200 years ago. You needed to get a message to your cousin Jane, who lived many miles away. You couldn't call Jane on your telephone, because phones hadn't been invented yet. You couldn't e-mail her. You couldn't send her a text message. How would you contact Jane?

You would write her a letter, of course!

A letter is a written message from one person (or group) to another. For hundreds of years, letters were the only way for people in distant places to communicate with each other.

Today we can communicate in lots of ways, but letters are still important. We read or write letters nearly every day—at work, at play, and everywhere in between.

To learn more about letters, keep reading!

Sincerely,

Nancy Loewen

Nancy Loewen
Author

3

Most of the letters we write fall into two groups: business and friendly. We write business letters to people we don't know, so it's important to follow the rules. We write friendly letters to people we know well, so we can be less formal.

Most letters have five basic parts: heading, greeting, body, closing, and signature/signature line. We'll be using these terms in the pages ahead, so take a good look at the following example.

123 Kangaroo Lane
Parade City, ND 54321
March 13, 2010

Paula Prince
Write Now Magazine
357 Fair Street
Bellington, ME 01234

HEADING
(your address, the date, and the address of your reader)

Dear Ms. Prince:

GREETING
(also called the salutation)

I would like to enter three poems in your Poems for a Crazy Day contest. The poems are enclosed. (I'm sorry about the grape juice stains on "Know No, Gnu." It was my little sister's fault.)

Sincerely,

CLOSING

Lucy Rickles

Lucy Rickles

BODY
(also called the main text)

SIGNATURE/ SIGNATURE LINE

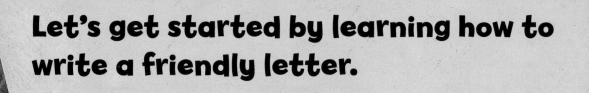

Let's get started by learning how to write a friendly letter.

~ Tool 1 ~

In a friendly letter, the **HEADING** has two parts: your address and the date. However, if you're writing to a really close friend or family member, you don't need to include your address. In that case, all you need is the date.

~ Tool 2 ~

The most common **GREETING** is "Dear," with the name followed by a comma. But if you know the reader really well, you can open your letter however you want. Sound like yourself!

Hey, Joe!
Yo, Joe.
Hi,
Dude!

3 Gray Duck Row
Bunnydale, KY 44444
March 27, 2010

Dear Joe,

~ Tool 3 ~

The **BODY** of a friendly letter should sound like you're talking. You can write about the things that are happening in your life. You should also show that you're interested in the other person's life. Ask questions, and you'll be more likely to get a letter back in return.

3 Gray Duck Row
Bunnydale, KY 44444
March 27, 2010

Dear Joe,

Guess what? I'm coming to see you! My parents say we can spend a few days in Chicago on our summer vacation. I can't wait.

How is your new school? Have you made some new friends? Everyone in Mr. Glidden's class really misses you.

Your tater-tot-tower record still stands. Mike tried to break it yesterday, but the tater tots fell down when he burped.

Write back soon!

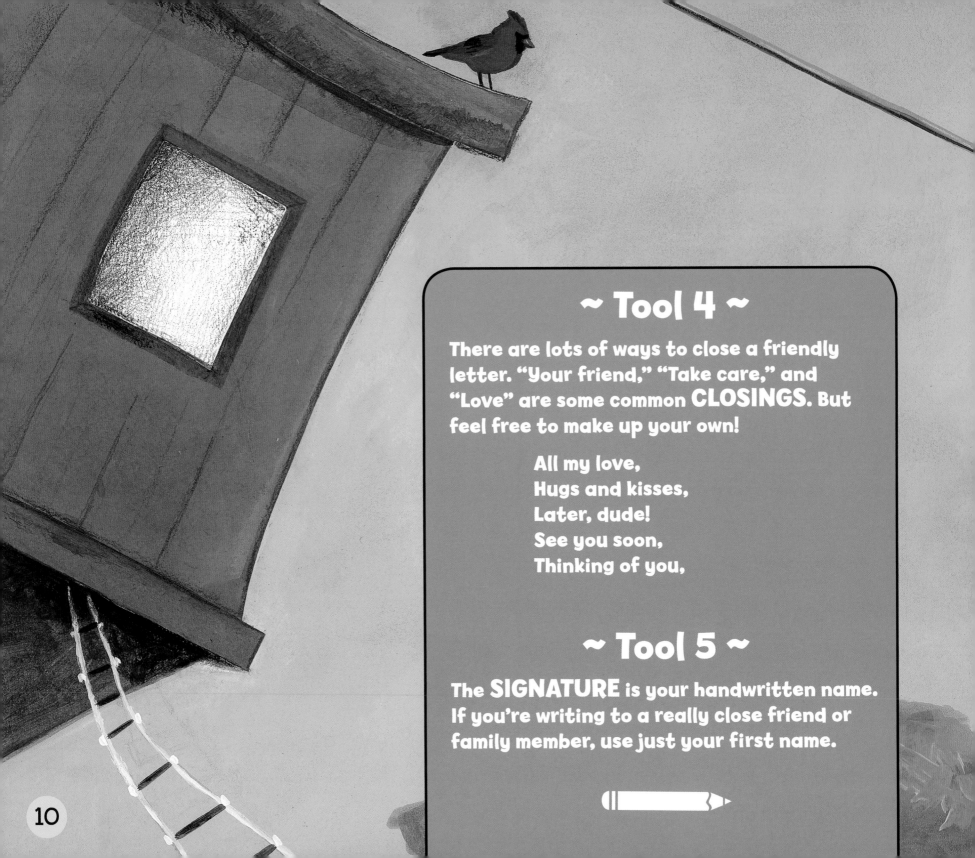

~ Tool 4 ~

There are lots of ways to close a friendly letter. "Your friend," "Take care," and "Love" are some common **CLOSINGS**. But feel free to make up your own!

All my love,
Hugs and kisses,
Later, dude!
See you soon,
Thinking of you,

~ Tool 5 ~

The **SIGNATURE** is your handwritten name. If you're writing to a really close friend or family member, use just your first name.

3 Gray Duck Row
Bunnydale, KY 44444
March 27, 2010

Dear Joe,

Guess what? I'm coming to see you! My parents say we can spend a few
days in Chicago on our summer vacation. I can't wait.

How is your new school? Have you made some new friends? Everyone in
Mr. Glidden's class really misses you.

Your tater-tot-tower record still stands. Mike tried to break it yesterday,
but the tater tots fell down wh

Write back soon!

Your friend,

Sam

Often, friendly letters are just about staying in touch. But we also use friendly letters to show our feelings about special situations.

Thank you notes are friendly letters, too. So are get well cards. These letters don't need to be long. But you should include a few details to show your reader that you've put some thought into it.

Dear Brad,

Thank you for coming to my birthday party. It was great to see you. Thanks for the metal detector, too. I've already found two quarters, an old pop can, and something else I can't identify. I can't wait to see what I find next!

Thanks again,

Zach

~ Tool 6 ~

PROOFREADING is important no matter what kind of letter you're writing. Pay attention to your spelling, punctuation, and grammar. A sloppy letter tells the reader that you were in a hurry, or that you didn't care.

14

Dear Amanda,

I'm sorry you broke your leg. That must have hurt! It's too bad you had to miss your hockey tournament. I hope you feel better soon.

Love,

Margie

~ Tool 7 ~

After you've finished your letter, you might remember something else you wanted to say. Do you have to start all over? No! A **POSTSCRIPT** is a sentence or short paragraph added to the end of a letter, after the signature. Use the initials *P.S.*, and then add what you want.

Dear Amanda,

I'm sorry you broke your leg. That must have hurt! It's too bad you had to miss your hockey tournament. I hope you feel better soon.

Love,

Margie

P.S. Can I sign your cast?

Now, let's move on to business letters!

ALFALFA AVE

In a business letter, the **HEADING** has three parts: your address, the date, and the name and address of your reader.

101 Clover Lane
Mudville, WA 99999
October 6, 2010

Norah Brown
101 Alfalfa Avenue
Splashville, ID 88888

~ Tool 2 ~

The **GREETING** of a business letter usually begins with "Dear." If you're writing to a man, use "Mr." If you're writing to a woman, use "Ms." If you know the woman is married, you can use "Mrs." Then add the person's last name and a colon.

What if you don't know the person's name? Use one of these greetings:

Dear Sir:
Dear Madam:
Dear Sir or Madam:
To Whom It May Concern:

101 Clover Lane
Mudville, WA 99999
October 6, 2010

Norah Brown
101 Alfalfa Avenue
Splashville, ID 88888

Dear Ms. Brown:

~ Tool 3 ~

The **BODY** of a business letter should be polite and to the point. If you are asking the reader to do something, be sure to include all of the information he or she will need.

In the letter on the opposite page, the writer states who she is. She explains how she heard of Ms. Brown. She quickly comes to the point of her letter, which is to ask for an interview. She gives her dad's name and phone number. And she does all of this in a very polite way.

101 Clover Lane
Mudville, WA 99999
October 6, 2010

Norah Brown
101 Alfalfa Avenue
Splashville, ID 88888

Dear Ms. Brown:

My name is Susan, and I'm in fourth grade at Grainwood Elementary. I read in the newspaper that you raise goats. Last month you won an award for your homemade goat cheese. Congratulations!

I am researching goats. May I talk to you about my project? Please call my father, Jeff, if you would like to set up an interview. Our number is 555-879-2241.

Thank you!

~ Tool 4 ~

"Sincerely" is a good **CLOSING** for a business letter. The word *sincerely* means "honestly and truthfully." But there are many other ways to close a business letter. Any of these closings would work:

Best wishes,
Cordially,
Regards,
With warm wishes,
Respectfully,

~ Tool 5 ~

The **SIGNATURE LINE** appears below your signature. It is simply your name. Use your first and last name. If you want, you can use your middle name, too.

If you are writing your business letter by hand, you should still include a signature line. Print your name, then sign above it.

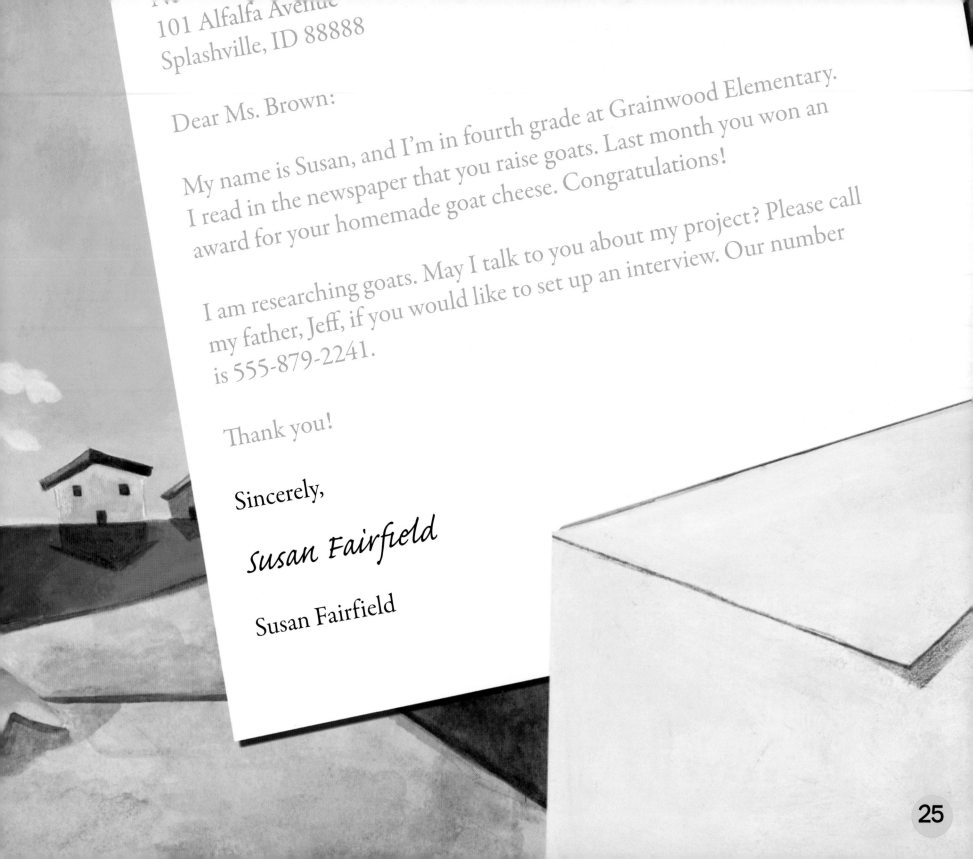

101 Alfalfa Avenue
Splashville, ID 88888

Dear Ms. Brown:

My name is Susan, and I'm in fourth grade at Grainwood Elementary. I read in the newspaper that you raise goats. Last month you won an award for your homemade goat cheese. Congratulations!

I am researching goats. May I talk to you about my project? Please call my father, Jeff, if you would like to set up an interview. Our number is 555-879-2241.

Thank you!

Sincerely,

Susan Fairfield

Susan Fairfield

~ Tool 8 ~

If you're sending a letter in the mail, you'll need to address an **ENVELOPE**.

Your name and address go in the upper left corner. This is called the return address. If your letter can't be delivered, it will be returned to you.

Your reader's name and address go in the middle of the envelope.

The stamp goes in the upper right corner.

Susan Fairfield
101 Clover Lane
Mudville, WA 99999

Norah Brown
101 Alfalfa Avenue
Splashville, ID 88888

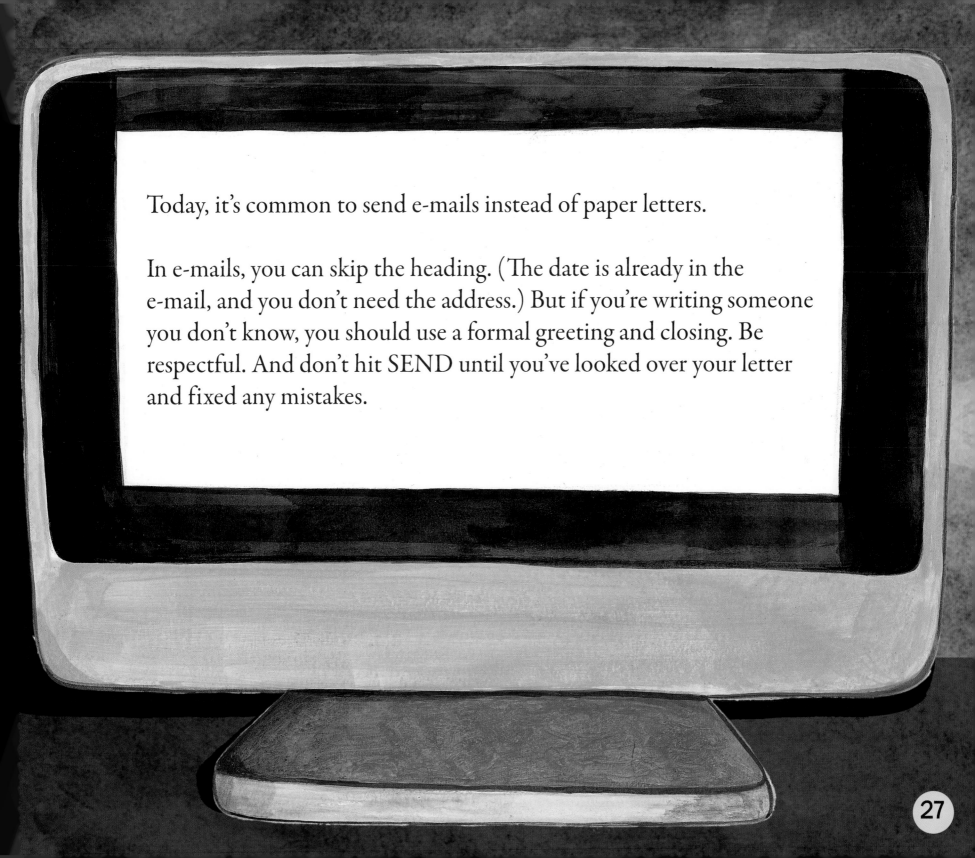

Today, it's common to send e-mails instead of paper letters.

In e-mails, you can skip the heading. (The date is already in the e-mail, and you don't need the address.) But if you're writing someone you don't know, you should use a formal greeting and closing. Be respectful. And don't hit SEND until you've looked over your letter and fixed any mistakes.

Let's Review!

These are the **8 tools** you need to write great letters.

The HEADING **(1)** answers the questions Who, Where, and When. In a friendly letter, the heading has two parts. In a business letter, it has three.

The GREETING **(2)** is a polite way to get started. It's like saying "hello."

The BODY **(3)** answers the questions What and Why. The body gives your reason for writing. In a business letter, the body should be to the point. If you are asking for something, be sure to give the reader all of the information he or she will need to help you.

The CLOSING **(4)** lets your reader know that you're almost done. Like the greeting, it's a way of being polite. The SIGNATURE and SIGNATURE LINE **(5)** let the reader know who wrote the letter.

PROOFREADING **(6)** helps you catch spelling and grammar mistakes.

The initials *P.S.* stand for POSTSCRIPT **(7)**. They bring attention to the fact that you're adding something to the letter.

Addressing the ENVELOPE **(8)** correctly is very important. You don't want your terrific letter to get lost in the mail!

Getting Started Exercises

- Pick out two characters in a favorite book. Pretend you are those characters, and have them write to each other about a problem they face in the story. What sorts of words would they use?

- Ask your parents or teachers if you can take part in a pen-pal program. You can make friends all around the world.

- Join a fan club, and write a letter to your favorite celebrity. Maybe you'll get a letter back!

- Do you feel strongly about something that's happening in your school? Write a letter to a school board member, and explain your thoughts.

Writing Tips

 Think of a letter as a little bit of YOU, going out into the world. The way you write should show how you would act if the person were right beside you. Would you hug that person or shake hands? Would you shout and laugh or would you use a quieter voice? Would you make jokes or talk politely?

 If you're writing a letter by hand, write a practice one first. When you're happy with what you've written, take a new piece of paper and rewrite the letter neatly.

 Have someone else look at your letter before you send it. Other people might see mistakes that you didn't notice.

 The best way to get really good at writing letters is to practice! You can write to your faraway friends and family. You can even write to people you see every day.

Glossary

body—the main part of a letter

closing—the end of a letter

communicate—to pass along thoughts, feelings or information

cordially—friendly, warmly

formal—official and proper

grammar—rules about using words

greeting—the beginning of a letter

heading—the part of a letter that includes the writer's and reader's addresses and the date

postscript—a message or note added after the writer's signature; *P.S.* stands for "postscript"

proofread—to read to find and fix mistakes

punctuation—marks used to make written language clear

regards—to show respect

signature—the writer's handwritten name

signature line—the writer's typed name below his or her signature

To Learn More

More Books to Read

Fletcher, Ralph. *How to Write Your Life Story*. New York: HarperCollins, 2007.

McElroy, Lisa Tucker. *Love, Lizzie: Letters to a Military Mom*. Morton Grove, Ill.: Albert Whitman & Company, 2005.

Roy, Jennifer Rozines, and Sherri Mabry Gordon. *You Can Write a Business Letter*. Berkeley Heights, N.J.: Enslow Publishers, 2003.

Summers, Jean. *The Kids' Guide to Writing Great Thank-You Notes*. Cranston, R.I.: Writers Collective, 2006.

On the Web

FactHound offers a safe, fun way to find educator-approved Internet sites related to this book.

Here's what you do:

1. Visit *www.facthound.com*
2. Choose your grade level.
3. Begin your search.

This book's ID number is 9781404853386

Look for all of the books in the Writer's Toolbox series:

Once Upon a Time: Writing Your Own Fairy Tale
Show Me a Story: Writing Your Own Picture Book
Sincerely Yours: Writing Your Own Letter
Words, Wit, and Wonder: Writing Your Own Poem